The Lost Railways of Essex
Neil Burgess

Canning Town Station *c.* 1900. It ceased to be a railway station in 2006 and is now a transport hub serving the Underground, the Docklands Light Railway and local buses.

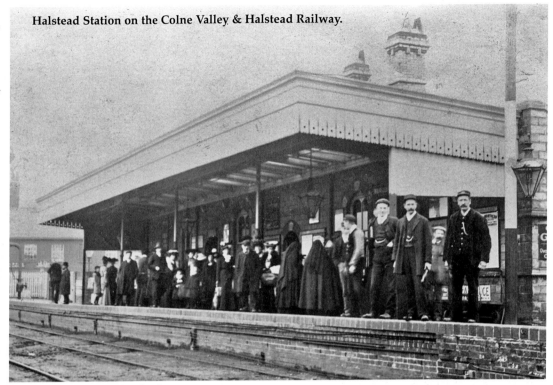

Halstead Station on the Colne Valley & Halstead Railway.

Acknowledgements

I am grateful to my friend and fellow railway historian Richard Morton for his work in checking the main text of this book and suggesting various alterations and corrections.
The publishers wish to thank the following for contributing photographs to this book: John Alsop for the front and back covers, and also the inside front and back covers as well as pages 1, 2, 4, 7, 9, 10, 11, 13, 14, 15, 17, 18, 19, 22, 25, 28, 30, 31, 36, 37, 39, 44, 45, 46, 47, 48, 49, 50, 51 and 53; and Richard Casserley for pages 8, 16, 20, 21, 23, 26, 27, 29, 34, 35, 38, 40, 41, 42, 43, 52, 54, 55 and 56.

Closure Dates

This book lists dates when stations and lines were closed to regular scheduled passenger traffic. Readers need to recognise that sources vary in deciding closure dates, some giving the last day on which regular services operated, others the first day when closure was effected and no passenger traffic operated. Especially on lines with no regular Sunday service, this might yield a discrepancy of two days depending on the method used. In some cases, particularly before the mid-1960s, stations along closed lines might be left substantially intact and periodically excursion trains called to pick up or set down passengers. In some areas unadvertised workmen's services were also run. Where sources indicate that this happened it may be noted in the text, but it does not affect the official closure date.

Introduction

Essex is a county which many people think they know, even if they have never actually visited it; it is probably associated in popular imagination with the urban and industrial strip of land reaching out from east London along the north bank of the Thames, a place of car factories, oil refineries, warehouses and commuter housing. As always, the reality is different. The greater part of the county is not urban at all, being made up of rolling countryside punctuated with villages and small towns such as Saffron Walden, as picturesque and historic as any in England. Agriculture and horticulture are important industries, even if today they employ relatively few people. Though there are no coal measures, there is plenty of mineral wealth in the form of gravel and aggregates found in the land reclaimed over the centuries from the sea and the river estuary, along which are to be found marshes and open spaces which certainly do not feel as though they are only a matter of a few dozen miles from central London. In the south of the county are historic towns, including the cathedral city of Chelmsford and the capital of Roman Britain, Colchester.

Paradoxically it is in the south of the county, and particularly in the land forming the northern bank of the Thames and its immediate hinterland, that the greater part of Essex's population now lives; paradoxically because before the Victorian age this would seem the least hospitable place in which to live, being very much a landscape of marsh and low-lying grassland. Two significant factors changed the face of southern Essex, these being its proximity to London, in the nineteenth century the greatest political and financial centre in the world, and the availability of the means to drain the marsh and convert it for use as a site for industry and population. Prior to the 1960s London was a great industrial city and many of its diverse industries, including engineering, shipbuilding and all kinds of manufacturing, found themselves constrained by the tightly-packed city around them. They moved outwards onto what might today be called 'greenfield sites', but were also joined by other and newer industries such as oil refining and motor vehicle manufacturing, both staples of post-1920s' Essex.

The twentieth century also saw great movements of people out from east London, an area associated in the Victorian consciousness with dirt, squalor and disease, in search of new and better places to live. The London County Council, armed with new powers from 1919, constructed huge estates of council-owned rented housing along the Thames, particularly in Dagenham, where Henry Ford had established his motor vehicle works, and Becontree. It has to be said that these early estates were not always the best of places to live, despite being clean and modern; too many people found them lonely and isolated compared with their former homes, but they set the growing trend for people living outside of the capital and travelling in for their daily work. To do so they needed frequent and reliable public transport, preferably at economical fares. The commuted charge ticket, offering a discount over a daily purchase in return for a lump-sum weekly, monthly or quarterly payment, gave rise to its users being described as 'commuters'. In the early twentieth century railways were the only means of transporting large numbers of people quickly and easily – as, in many ways, they still are. The trend has changed throughout the century, but has not abated; this has secured the existence of many of the county's railway routes and so too has the development of seaside resorts like Walton-on-the-Naze, Clacton and Southend, geared particularly to the day visitors who have filled so many trains out of London over the years.

Away from the urban centres of south Essex, railways have fared less well. In many places this has been because they have cut across the grain of the heavily used routes radiating out from London, serving a much more local area and often easy prey for the motor bus, lorry and, latterly, for the private car. Some lines, such as the Elsenham & Thaxted Light Railway, simply appeared on the scene too late to make the impact on the local economy their promoters hoped for. However, even London Transport's electrified network was not immune to falling receipts: witness the fate of the Epping to Ongar section of the Central line.

Even so, Essex's railway network has fared better than that of other counties and due to increasing road congestion, along with fresh thinking about the dangers of pollution and conservation of scarce resources like oil, they look likely to go on serving the needs of the population of this part of the country. Even if some of the more picturesque lines have long gone, there is still much to see and use.

Audley End – Bartlow

Passenger service withdrawn 7 September 1964
Distance 7 ¼ miles
Companies Saffron Walden Railway

Stations closed	*Date of closure*
Acrow Halt *	7 September 1964
Ashdon Halt	7 September 1964

Stations closed	*Date of closure*
Saffron Walden	7 September 1964

* Opened on 25 March 1957.

Saffron Walden Station.

Saffron Walden is one of the ancient market towns of north-east Essex, established as a centre for cloth-making from the Middle Ages. When the main line from London to Cambridge was built, it ran through the nearby town of Audley End to take advantage of the lie of the land, but thereby missed Saffron Walden. It was left to local initiative to propose and construct a railway to serve the town, the plan being to construct a link between the London – Cambridge line at Audley End and the Cambridge – Colchester line (see *Suffolk's Lost Railways*) at Bartlow on the Essex – Suffolk border. The Saffron Walden Railway obtained its parliamentary Act in 1862, assistance being offered to the project by the Great Eastern – paradoxically, the unwillingness of the GE's predecessor, the Eastern Counties, to build a line had resulted in the local company's formation. Construction was hardly swift, the one and three quarter miles from Audley End to Saffron Walden opening on 21 November 1865; the remaining five and a half miles to Bartlow following in October 1866.

Despite being a single company's route, the Saffron Walden Railway was effectively operated as two lines, the short section from Audley End to Saffron Walden having the most frequent service. The independent company was acquired by the Great Eastern in 1877 and from then until 1894 Saffron Walden enjoyed a daily through service to Liverpool Street. The line was lightly constructed and this prevented the use of larger main-line locomotives, though from time to time the route was used as a diversion if there were engineering works on the Cambridge main line. It is thought that the London through service ended in 1894 because the venerable locomotives used to haul the trains were withdrawn!

For much of its life thereafter the passenger services were operated using push-pull trains, often comprised of ancient coaches handed down from main line services. When these were eventually pensioned off their replacements were four-wheeled railbuses, but they failed to make significant increases in the passenger numbers, not least because many commuters for London drove to Audley End to catch their trains rather than using the branch. Unsurprisingly, the Beeching Report listed the branch for closure, which was effected in September 1964.

Beckton Junction – Gallions

Passenger service withdrawn	29 December 1940 *	*Stations closed*	*Date of closure*
Distance	1 ¾ miles	Beckton Central	29 December 1940
Companies	Royal Albert Dock Company	Manor Way	29 December 1940
		Gallions	29 December 1940
Stations closed	*Date of closure*		
Connaught Road	29 December 1940	* Actually discontinued from September (see text).	

During the nineteenth century London was not only an important trading port but also a significant passenger destination, much as it had been for centuries before. The creation of the Victorian port of London resulted in the building of several passenger ports along to lower reaches of the Thames, one of which was at Gallions, to the east of Canning Town, which boasted not only facilities for embarkation and disembarkation, but also a hotel for travellers. In order to ensure easy access to the main line railway network, the Royal Albert Dock Company constructed a passenger-carrying railway line from Albert Dock Junction on the Great Eastern's North Woolwich line to Gallions. Opened throughout in July 1881, it was worked by the Great Eastern from June 1896 and the company provided a frequent passenger service, though one which diminished gradually with the passage of the years and changing patterns of travel. The dock company staffed the line and the 1922 edition of Bradshaw indicated that the service was officially provided by the Port of London Authority. By the outbreak of war in 1939 the service was much reduced, but even this ceased when, on 7 September 1940, the line was severed by bombing of the docks. The service was at first officially suspended, but withdrawn permanently with effect from 29 December in the same year. Goods services continued until October 1950.

Bishop's Stortford – Braintree

Passenger service withdrawn	3 March 1952	*Stations closed*	*Date of closure*
Distance	18 miles	Felsted ****	3 March 1952
Companies	Bishop's Stortford, Dunmow & Braintree Railway *	Bannister Green Halt ***	3 March 1952
		Rayne	3 March 1952
Stations closed	*Date of closure*	Braintree (first station)	22 February 1869
Hockerill Halt **	3 March 1952		
Stane Street Halt ***	3 March 1952	* Actually opened by the Great Eastern Railway (see text).	
Takeley	3 March 1952	** Opened in 1910.	
Easton Lodge	3 March 1952	*** Opened on 18 December 1922.	
Dunmow	3 March 1952	**** Originally named Felstead until 5 June 1950.	

As related in the Witham – Maldon section, that line was originally built so as to continue across the Eastern Counties Railway main line to reach Braintree, the section opening in 1848. This meant that Braintree became the railhead for the more important town of Dunmow, along with Bishop's Stortford, through which the Eastern & Northern Railway's line from London to Cambridge had opened in 1842. There were several proposals for lines to pass through Dunmow, not least the main line of the Great Northern Railway in the 1840s, but they came to nothing. It was left to local interests, promoting the Bishop's Stortford, Dunmow & Braintree Railway, which secured its parliamentary Act in 1861, to attempt to construct a line to the town. The original intention was to construct a passenger and goods line between the towns in the company's title along with a goods branch from Dunmow to Epping; in the event the first was built, but not the second and this may well have adversely affected the prospects of the line.

Hockerill Halt.

Takeley Station, September 1962.

Long before any trains ran, the BSD&BR was in financial difficulties. In 1865, a year after construction began, the company faced ruin and was bought out by the Eastern Counties Railway which completed the construction and opened the line on 22 February 1869. The original station in Braintree became the goods depot and a second passenger station was opened for the now through line to Witham. However, as noted in the Witham – Maldon section, the two appear to have been operated separately, the Bishops Stortford – Braintree line having five daily return journeys in 1922 and the Braintree – Witham line ten.

There was some through passenger traffic, mainly in the form of excursions to the Essex coast, but little else. The line's traffic was mainly agricultural, though the Great Eastern opened Hockerill Halt in 1910 to serve a local golf club and later, in 1922, Bannister Green and Stane Street. In the years after the Great War the government's wish to develop home produced sugar from beet, rather than continue to rely on imported cane sugar, was to have a significant effect on the eastern counties of England where soil and weather conditions favoured beet cultivation. A sugar refining factory at Felstead made extensive use of rail transport for many years, the beet campaign in the autumn producing a great deal of traffic for this, and many other rural railways. Goods traffic was reasonable, aided by new industries in Braintree.

Dunmow Station.

Passenger services, which in 1946 were four return journeys daily plus a return working between Bishops Stortford and Dunmow only, did not prosper and became an early post-war casualty, ending in March 1952. As related elsewhere, Braintree reverted to being a terminus on the line from Witham and still is today. The Beeching Report of 1963 considered goods services worth retaining, but they dwindled in the following years; the section from Felstead to Dunmow closed completely on 18 December 1966, the line being progressively closed back to Bishop's Stortford by 1 March 1972.

Bannister Green Halt.

Canning Town – North Woolwich

Passenger service withdrawn	29 May 1994	*Stations closed*	*Date of closure*
Distance	3 miles	Silverton **	29 May 1994
Companies	North Woolwich Railway	North Woolwich	29 May 1994

Stations closed	*Date of closure*
Victoria Docks Tidal Basin *	14 August 1943
Victoria Docks Custom House	29 May 1994

* Both Tidal Basin and Custom House were prefaced ÔVictoria Docks' in timetables, though not necessarily on the stations themselves.
** Silverton was latterly named Silverton & London City Airport before closure.

Silverton Station.

The line to North Woolwich is a good example of speculative development, in this case promoted by G. P. Bidder who had built a number of lines in the Greater London area, including the Wimbledon & Croydon. At the time of its authorisation in 1845, this part of the Essex marshes were almost wholly uninhabited and sceptics dubbed the North Woolwich Railway 'Bidder's Folly'. It opened to passengers on 14 June 1847 and in the first seven years of its existence Bidder operated the trains himself. It was bought by the Eastern Counties & Thames Junction Railway in the year of its opening, the latter company providing the connection with the Eastern Counties line via Stratford. A connection from the London, Tilbury & Southend line east of Bromley was opened to the North Woolwich line in 1858.

Bidder was not content with just a piece of railway; he bought up tracts of marsh and constructed the Victoria Dock on them, turning the area into a major centre for shipping. The creation of the dock caused a realignment of the NWR, the line now skirting the north side of the dock while the old route served dockside industries. A line was constructed to Beckton, branching off the North Woolwich line at Tidal Basin in 1880, though this closed as a result of wartime damage in 1943.

Train services to North Woolwich were provided during the later part of the nineteenth century by the Great Eastern, into whose network the NWR was absorbed; between 1866 and 1874 the North London Railway had shared services with the Great Eastern. The Great Eastern operated trains to North Woolwich from Liverpool Street, but it was also served by workings from the Palace Gates line. Surprisingly the route maintained its passenger trains until 1994, though there are plans to reinstate the service and extend the line under the Thames to link up with the Blackheath – Slade Green line as part of the Crossrail network. Planned completion is scheduled for 2017.

Chappel & Wakes Colne – Haverhill

Passenger service withdrawn	1 January 1962 *
Distance	18 ½ miles
Companies	Colne Valley & Halstead Railway

Stations closed	*Date of closure*
White Colne **	1 January 1962
Earls Colne ***	1 January 1962
Halstead	1 January 1962
Sible & Castle Hedingham ****	1 January 1962
Yeldham	1 January 1962
Whitley	10 May 1863
Birdbrook	1 January 1962
Haverhill South	14 July 1924

* Some sources quote 30 December 1961 but most likely 1 January 1962 was the day on which the closure became effective, i.e. the first day without trains.

** Originally named Colne Station, which closed on 1 May 1889. Reopened as White Colne on 1 April 1908.

*** Originally named Ford Gate until renamed Colne on 1 May 1889; renamed Earls Colne on 1 May 1905.

**** Originally named Castle Hedingham until September 1867. Reopened as part of the Colne Valley Heritage Railway in 1973.

Temporary station, replaced by Birdbrook.

Originally named Haverhill until 1 July 1923.

White Colne Station, May 1956.

Earls Colne Station.

This short line, which managed to retain its independence up to the Grouping of 1923, was a further Essex byway of the kind beloved of railway enthusiasts, even if not always fully appreciated by passengers. Unlike the Kelvedon & Tollesbury and the Elsenham & Thaxted, the Colne Valley was not a product of the Light Railways Act but a fully fledged company with origins dating back to an Act of Parliament of June 1856 which authorised the construction of a line from a junction with the Eastern Counties Railway at Chappel to the town of Halstead.

Halstead Station.

The original intention of running into the Eastern Counties' station hung in the balance for a while as a result of less than amicable relations between the two companies; but these were resolved before the CV&H opened on 16 April 1860. Hardly had trains begun running when the company embarked upon a thirteen-mile extension from Halsted to Haverhill, which opened throughout on 10 May 1863. The little company was the first to reach Haverhill; the Great Eastern, which had emerged out of amalgamations that included the Eastern Counties in 1862, opened their line through the town in 1865.

Despite the presence of the Great Eastern at both ends, the Colne Valley managed not only to remain independent but to cultivate good relations with its greater neighbour. The CV&H owned its own locomotives and rolling stock and undertook its own running repairs at Haverhill until 1906 when these were concentrated on Halstead; but the Great Eastern took responsibility for more extensive work at Stratford. The little company weathered difficult financial times during the mid 1870s and enjoyed reasonable prosperity in the years around the turn of the nineteenth century, but it can hardly have been a goldmine for investors. Nonetheless it was much loved, even when merged into the London & North Eastern Railway in 1923.

Sible & Castle Hedingham Station, May 1956.

The Second World War saw an upsurge of traffic in connection with the US Army Air Force bases in the area, but gradual decline accompanied the peace and the usual search for economies during the 1950s saw the introduction of multiple-unit diesel trains. There were an assortment of industries along the line including agricultural machinery makers, brickworks at Castle Hedingham, Courtauld's silk mills at Halstead, and flour mills and tanneries.

Agricultural produce also made up the goods receipts, but in the post-war world these gradually ebbed away either because the industries declined or because those which survived used road transport. Passenger services ended in January 1962 – something for which Dr Beeching cannot be blamed – and goods ceased completely on 19 April 1965.

The track was lifted and buildings demolished, but this was not the end of the Colne Valley & Halstead. In 1973 a mile of track was reinstated near Castle Hedingham by a group of enthusiasts intent on preserving the line as a steam railway. It remains in operation today, keeping the memory and reality of the line alive for future generations.

Corringham – Corytown

Passenger service withdrawn   3 March 1952   *Stations closed*   *Date of closure*
Distance   2 ¾ miles   Corringham   3 March 1952
Companies   Corringham Light Railway   Corytown *   3 March 1952

* Sometimes listed as Coryton. Originally named Kynochtown until some time between 1919 and 1923.

Corringham Station.

The marshes along the Thames estuary have provided sites for a range of industries over the years, but one of the more unusual was the manufacture of explosives from the latter part of the nineteenth century until after the Great War. In 1896 the Birmingham firm of G. Kynoch & Company selected a spot on the marshes near Shellhaven Creek for the construction of an explosives factory, the site providing easy transportation for the finished product by river to the Royal Arsenal at Woolwich as well as a location sufficiently remote from built-up areas in case of accidents. Because of its remoteness, Kynoch & Co. undertook to build a small settlement for the 600 employees at the factory and their families, the location being named Kynochtown. The factory and settlement were served by a standard gauge light railway, connected to the London, Tilbury & Southend Railway's Thames Haven branch off the Tilbury Town – Pitsea section of their main line.

Kynochtown Station, before it was renamed Coryton.

The Corringham Light Railway opened in 1901, first carrying passengers from 22 June. It was mainly used by Kynoch's employees but also carried public passengers travelling to other industrial locations in the area. As well as supplies for Kynoch's factory it carried coal and bricks, the latter made near Corringham. There were originally six return passenger workings daily and traffic of all kinds increased rapidly after the outbreak of war in August 1914. Once the war ended traffic reduced equally quickly and the Kynoch factory was sold to the fuel dealers Cory Brothers of Cardiff. They converted the factory site into an oil storage plant, retaining the employees' housing settlement and renaming it Corytown (or Coryton) some time between 1919 and 1923. Road developments reduced passenger use of the railway, though the service managed to survive the Second World War and eventually ended in March 1952. Goods traffic continued until 1957, latterly under the auspices of the Vacuum Oil Company, later Mobil, which had bought the plant from Cory Brothers in 1950.

Custom House – Beckton

Passenger service withdrawn	29 December 1940	*Stations closed*	*Date of closure*
Distance	1 ¾ miles	Beckton	29 December 1940 *
Companies	Gas Light & Coke Company		

* Some sources quote 28 December.

This single-track branch was constructed by the Gas Light & Coke Company to service their large gas works by the Thames at Beckton. Goods traffic began on 14 October 1872 and a workmen's passenger service was instituted from 17 March 1874. Like the nearby Gallions branch, the Beckton line was operated by the Great Eastern. The passenger service was never frequent and ceased from 29 December 1940, though goods traffic continued for many years afterwards.

Elsenham – Thaxted

Passenger service withdrawn	15 September 1952	*Stations closed*	*Date of closure*
Distance	5 ½ miles	Mill Road Halt	15 September 1952
Companies	Elsenham & Thaxted Light Railway	Henham Halt	15 September 1952
		Sibley's for Chickney & Broxtead	15 September 1952
Stations closed	*Date of closure*	Cutler's Green Halt	15 September 1952
Elsenham (light railway station)	15 September 1952	Thaxted	15 September 1952

No. 68530 with the 4.00 p.m. from Thaxted at Elsenham Station, June 1951.

Sibley's for Chickney & Broxted Station, August 1952.

This short line was another child of the 1896 Light Railways Act, being promoted to open up a tract of countryside around Thaxted, but also to continue to Great Bardfield. In the event Thaxted was as far as the line got, so it proved to be only half its projected mileage. In truth there was little hard financial support from the local area for the line and most of the money to build it came from the Great Eastern and the Treasury. Although authorised in 1906, it was to be five years before construction commenced and seven until the line opened on 1 April 1913. This really was a case of arriving on the scene at the eleventh hour and the economic and social climate which emerged after the Great War took its toll on many longer-established and financially sounder undertakings than this small line tucked away in the byways of rural Essex.

The line was constructed as cheaply as possible, the intermediate stations being very spartan in their facilities and the terminus at Thaxted being some distance from the town in order to save the cost of bridging the river; the 1922 timetable proclaimed it to be 'station for Great Bardfield'. As noted in the Kelvedon – Tollesbury section, light railways often operated mixed trains in which goods wagons were conveyed behind the passenger coaches. Though this was convenient to the operating staff, passengers' journeys were often lengthened by the need to wait while wagons were attached to, or detached from, the train at wayside stations. Neither of these realities helped fend off competition by buses and lorries. Seven trains a day in each direction plied the line in 1922, all but one connecting with trains to and from London at Elsenham, with an extra service on Saturdays. The London & North Eastern Railway timetable for 1946 showed four return journeys a day – during the war it had been only two – but it was clear that any search for railway economies by the newly created British Railways would be unlikely to pass it by. So it was that passenger services ceased on 15 September 1952, goods traffic surviving it for less than a year.

Epping – Ongar

Passenger service withdrawn	30 September 1994	*Stations closed*	*Date of closure*
Distance	6 ½ miles	North Weald	3 October 1994
Companies	Great Eastern Railway	Blake Hall	2 November 1981
		Ongar	3 October 1994

No. 67200 with the 4:18 p.m. from Ongar to Epping at North Weald Station, April 1957.

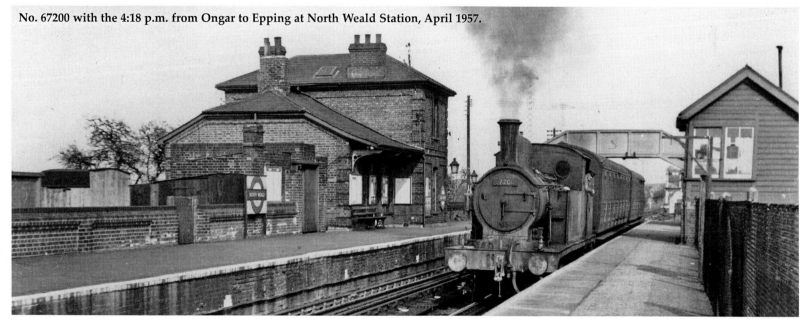

The railway between Epping and Chipping Ongar – usually known simply as Ongar – has had a long and complex history, which looks set to evolve for years to come. Its origins lie in the 1840s when plans were first made, by the London & Blackwall Railway, to construct a line out from the centre of London to the then rural district of Epping. The Eastern Counties Railway, under the control of George Hudson, was sufficiently concerned by the plan not only to refuse the L&B running rights into Liverpool Street but to take steps to construct a line of its own. So it was that in July 1853 the Eastern Counties' act received parliamentary consent for the construction of a line from Stratford to Loughton, which opened on 22 August 1856.

Three years later, a line from Loughton to Dunmow via Epping and Chipping Ongar was proposed by the Epping Railway. The Eastern Counties again took action, this time by gaining consent for the construction of the line from Braintree to Bishops Stortford via Dunmow, effectively blocking the Epping proposal, and then absorbing the company. Having seen off another potential rival the Great Eastern, created from the amalgamation of the Eastern Counties and Eastern Union railways, undertook the construction of an extension of its own from Loughton to Ongar via Epping. There was a possibility of a further extension, to join the main line to Chelmsford, but this never materialised. The line opened to Ongar, as the terminus was named, on 24 April 1865. The line had been constructed as single track beyond Loughton and was in time doubled as far as Epping, but remained single thereafter.

Blake Hall Station.

The line passed from the Great Eastern to the London & North Eastern in 1923 and remained as a relatively rural extension of an outer-suburban route. In the inter-war years the population of London began to spread further outwards into south Essex and with it developed the need for improved public transport. The creation of the London Passenger Transport Board in 1933 was intended to secure co-ordinated passenger provision for the capital and part of its programme included an extension of the Central Line of the underground from Liverpool Street to Epping, effectively a counterpart to the former Great Eastern surface line. The war put these plans into abeyance, but they were revived afterwards and the Central Line reached Loughton in 1948. There was an extensive programme of new housing in the Loughton area and thought was given to extending electrification beyond Loughton to Ongar, using the existing GER line. The electric service reached Epping in September 1949, services beyond being provided by steam-hauled push-pull trains operated by the Eastern Region of British Railways on behalf of the London Transport Executive (as the LPTB had become).

The goods yard with the station beyond it Ongar, *c.* 1900.

In the event, steam power remained the means of reaching Ongar until electrification was completed to that point, services beginning on 18 November 1957. Technical details of the electrification meant that through running to Ongar was not possible and passengers still had to change at Epping, as was the case with the steam service. Despite further new housing around Ongar, passenger numbers were not encouraging and London Transport began thinking of economies, including reducing the number of trains, from late 1966. In 1970 it proposed closure beyond Epping, which was averted only by Essex County Council agreeing to subsidise the service. The subsidy ended in 1977 and a further attempt at closure was narrowly defeated three years later. But the writing was on the wall and, despite an attempt to increase provision of services in 1989, closure finally came at the end of September 1994.

Yet the Epping – Ongar line was far from finished. After an unsuccessful attempt to run a service by a private company – their main contribution seems to have been the removal of the third and fourth electrified rails – the Epping Ongar Railway Volunteer Society started to operate passenger trains between Ongar and North Weald from October 2004. A further change of ownership followed in 2008, resulting in the line becoming a heritage railway operating preserved steam and diesel locomotives.

Kelvedon – Tollesbury

		Stations closed	Date of closure
Passenger service withdrawn	7 May 1951	Inworth	7 May 1951
Distance	10 ¼ miles	Tiptree	7 May 1951
Companies	Kelvedon & Tollesbury Light Railway	Tolleshunt Knights	7 May 1951
		Tolleshunt d'Arcy	7 May 1951
Stations closed	*Date of closure*	Tollesbury	7 May 1951
Kelvedon Low Level	7 May 1951	Tollesbury Pier	17 July 1921
Feering Halt	7 May 1951		

Kelvedon Low Level station.

Feering Halt, April 1957.

The Light Railways Act of 1896 was a measure intended to assist the building of railways in sparsely populated areas as an impetus to their development. Based on earlier legislation in Ireland, it recognised that lines promoted and paid for on purely commercial grounds were never going to be built in areas which might, by their presence, most benefit and it allowed local authorities to finance such schemes through public rates and also make grants towards their construction. Treasury grants were also available, but everything was founded on the need for an existing railway company to construct, and in most cases operate, such lines.

Thus it was that in May 1897 application was made to the Light Railway Commissioners – the 1896 Act allowed that permission need not take the form of an Act of Parliament – for the construction of a light railway from the Great Eastern London – Colchester line at Kelvedon to the small port of Tollesbury on the Blackwater estuary. For all that the process was intended to simplify and speed the construction of light railways, the Light Railway Order was not granted until January 1901 and building started two years later.

The station under construction at Tiptree. Curiously the name on the sign is Tiptree Heath.

When the line opened on 1 October 1904 there were four intermediate stations between Kelvedon and Tollesbury and the line continued beyond the town to Tollesbury Pier, a grandiose scheme having been discussed to create a major port there – railway promotions were prone to such flights of fancy. Between the wars the LNER added a further intermediate station between the wars at Feering, but by the time of the Grouping in 1923 the line to the pier had already closed.

The 6.37 p.m. from Tollesbury at Tiptree Station.

There were several staple traffics along the line, primarily fruit for Wilkin's jam and preserves factory at Tiptree, along with finished foodstuffs going out. Tollesbury landed quantities of seafood, which gave the light railway the nickname of the 'Crab and Winkle line'. The Great Eastern operated it from the outset and provided the locomotives and rolling stock.

Originally ordinary six-wheeled compartment coaches with extra steps down to the low-level platforms of the stations were employed, but after 1928 two bogie coaches from the Wisbech & Upwell line in Cambridgeshire were transferred to Essex after their own line lost its passenger service. These coaches were of the open saloon type with end platforms and steps; one achieved fame on the silver screen when used for making the Ealing comedy *The Titfield Thunderbolt* in 1952 and the other, having been used for many years as a store shed, is preserved.

Tollesbury Station, *c.* **1900.**

Trains were often mixed, that is, with goods wagons marshalled behind the passenger coaches, so there could be delays while wagons were picked up or dropped off along the route; since the Light Railway Order imposed a maximum speed of 25 miles per hour, progress was leisurely. Between the wars there were three return journeys a day, with five on Wednesdays and Saturdays, taking 31 minutes for eight and a quarter miles.

Surprisingly, the Kelvedon & Tollesbury survived the Second World War and continued to carry passengers until May 1951, the line being closed completely beyond Tiptree in October of that year. The remainder of the line continued to see goods traffic until October 1962.

Tollesbury Pier Station, *c.* **1910.**

Pier Station, Tollesbury.   Nº4.

Shelford – Haverhill – Sudbury *

Passenger service withdrawn	6 March 1967
Distance	31 ¼ miles
Companies	Colchester, Stour Valley, Sudbury & Halstead Railway

Stations closed	*Date of closure*
Bartlow	6 March 1967
Sturmer	6 March 1967

* Closed stations on this line that were in Cambridgeshire were Pampisford and Linton; Bartlow Station was also in Cambridgeshire, though the village is in Essex. Closed stations that were in Suffolk were Haverhill, Stoke, Clare, Cavendish, Glemsford, Long Melford, and Sudbury (first station). Hockerill Halt was in Hertfordshire.

Entering Bartlow Station, May 1957. The train approaching the junction on the right is on the Audley End – Bartlow line and is passing the platform of Bartlow Station on that line.

The Stour Valley line was a cross-country route linking Cambridge to Colchester and serving a series of textile-making towns along the way. The line left the main line to Liverpool Street at Shelford and traversed the country between Cambridgeshire, Suffolk and Essex, crossing and recrossing the county boundaries as it made for Long Melfold and Sudbury. Originally independent, the company was absorbed into the Great Eastern in August 1862.

Arriving at Bartlow Station are the 12.30 p.m. from Marks Tey to Cambridge, and the 1.26 p.m. from Cambridge to Colchester, July 1956.

At three points the line made junctions with branches, that from Bartlow serving Saffron Walden and joining the Cambridge – Liverpool Street main line at Audley End; while at Haverhill and again beyond Sudbury at Chappel & Wakes Colne connection was made with both ends of the independent Colne Valley & Halstead Railway, which largely duplicated that section of the Stour Valley line from across the county boundary in Essex.

Provision was made to convert the original single line to double track if required, though this never happened. It was a valuable alternative route east of Cambridge to either Ipswich or the Essex coastal resorts of Clacton and Walton-on-the-Naze. The Beeching Report of 1963 saw no future for it, either as a local or a diversionary route and it closed to goods between Shelford and Sudbury from 31 October 1966 and completely from 6 March the following year. The section from Sudbury to Marks Tey on the Colchester – Liverpool Street main line remains open.

Thames Haven Junction – Thames Haven

Passenger service withdrawn	1 October 1880	*Stations closed*	*Date of closure*
Distance	3 ½ miles	Stanford Road level crossing *	1955 (date uncertain)
Companies	Thames Haven Dock & Railway	Miners' Safety Explosives Co. works *	1955 (date uncertain)
		Thames Haven Station	1 October 1880

* Opened for the workmen's services in 1923 (see text)

Thames Haven Station.

For such a short piece of line, this one had a somewhat complex history. It was originally promoted in the Thames Haven Dock & Railway Act of 1836, under the powers of which the line and its associated dock were constructed. The London, Tilbury & Southend Railway bought the line, dock and an associated piece of land for a little under £50,000, ownership being transferred from 8 September 1855. The line had been opened for both passenger and goods traffic, though it seems clear that the LT&SR's prime interest was in the latter, since regular public passenger services ceased from 1 October 1880. However, occasional services continued to use the line in connection with river steamers until 1909; the pier they had used was removed in 1912.

Under an Act of 1886, the LT&SR gained powers to construct a spur to Thames Haven Wharf. Oil storage and refining plants were growing up along the Thames estuary and also at least one explosives factory. From 1 January 1923, the London, Midland & Scottish Railway – as successor to both the LT&SR and also the Midland Railway, which had absorbed it in 1912 – began running workmen's trains and halts were opened at Stanford Road level crossing and the Miners' Safety explosives works in connection with these. The services continued until some time during 1955. The line continues in use for goods traffic.

Tilbury Town – Tilbury Riverside

Passenger service withdrawn   28 November 1992
Distance   1 mile
Companies   London, Tilbury & Southend Railway

Stations closed   *Date of closure*
Tilbury Riverside *   28 November 1992

* Originally named Tilbury until 3 August 1934.

The platforms at Tilbury Station.

The London, Tilbury & Southend Railway was one of south-east England's more singular small companies, managing not only to return a tidy profit on its operations but to do so while managing to remain independent of its all-embracing neighbour, the Great Eastern Railway. In 1912 it was bought not by the GER but by the Midland, and so in 1923 became an outpost of that even greater railway empire, the London, Midland & Scottish.

The Interior of Tilbury Station, 1932.

The LT&SR ran along the north bank of the Thames estuary, serving the places in its title and providing a link for daily travellers – long before the term 'commuter' had been thought of – into and out of London. However, in the nineteenth century, travellers not only wished to travel alongside the river but also to cross it by means of various ferries running between the Essex and Kent shores. One such ferry connected Tilbury with Gravesend, a useful way of avoiding what would otherwise be a long and tedious land journey. Indeed many such ferries all around the country had existed long before the railways came, some dating back to the middle ages. Trading vessels also plied up and down the Thames, serving the towns and industries along the bank.

Tilbury Station and Pier from the Thames.

When the LT&SR line was projected to Tilbury in 1852, provision was made to run not only to Tilbury itself but to the river pier to connect with the Gravesend ferry. The line opened on 13 April 1854 and trains to and from Southend ran to the pier and then reversed to continue their journeys. In the 1880s there was a proposal to construct an underwater tunnel to replace the ferry, but nothing came of it. The 1922 timetable showed 34 trains connecting with ferries in each direction on weekdays, between 6.00 a.m. and midnight. Tilbury was also an important port for long-distance passenger carrying ships, avoiding the need to berth further up river and during the 1920s the London Midland & Scottish and the Port of London Authority opened a new landing stage at Tilbury to accommodate this traffic, underlining its importance.

Tilbury Town – Tilbury Riverside

Tilbury Station was rebuilt in the early thirties and this photograph from 1935 shows the redevelopment. The station hall prominent in previous pictures lies partially demolished in the centre of the picture. In the top left of the picture is the junction of the branch with the main line.

In the post-war era increased car ownership took its toll on river ferries just as it did on local railways; in particular the opening of the Dartford road tunnel in 1963 offered motorists a means of crossing the river further downstream than before and ferry traffic suffered accordingly. Even so, the short line to Tilbury Riverside, as it had become in 1936, survived until 28 November 1992. Paradoxically, the ferry which predated the railway has survived its closure.

Witham – Maldon

Passenger service withdrawn	7 September 1964	*Stations closed*	*Date of closure*
Distance	5 ¾ miles	Maldon East & Heybridge ***	7 September 1964
Companies	Eastern Counties Railway		

* Originally named Wickham until 1 October 1913.
** Originally named Langford until 1 July 1923.

Stations closed	*Date of closure*
Wickham Bishops *	7 September 1964
Langford & Ulting **	7 September 1964

*** Originally named Maldon until 1 October 1889; then named Maldon East until 1 October 1907.

Wickham Bishops Station, *c. 1915.*

Many early railway lines were intended to connect main centres of population and relatively little thought was given to serving smaller communities along or near the route. Particularly in the early years, promoters tended to assume that smaller places could be served by short-distance road journeys and there was often a marked unwillingness to sacrifice potentially more favourable alignments for the sake of detours to small towns. Thus it was that when the Eastern Counties Railway constructed its line from London to Colchester, which opened in 1843, it bypassed the town of Maldon, situated on the estuary of the River Blackwater and noted for the production of sea salt and its coastal trade in potatoes and grain.

Langford Station.
The only Station in England having a Station Mistress.

Langford Station, *c.* 1905.

Exclusion from the railway network encouraged local interests to promote a line of their own, the Maldon, Witham & Braintree Railway, linking Maldon with the Eastern Counties line at Witham, almost six miles away. The parliamentary bill, deposited in 1845, was for a line to continue north-westwards to Braintree, crossing the main line on the level. Fearing a prospective rival, the Eastern Counties took a financial interest in the project after parliamentary consent had been gained, construction beginning in 1847. The line opened from Maldon through Witham to Braintree on 2 October 1848, though it would appear that by the early years of the twentieth century at least the two sections either side of the main line were being operated separately.

Maldon Station, June 1938.

The line was later joined by a second branch to Maldon from Woodham Ferrers but the original route prospered more and lasted longer. Services increased through the twentieth century from seven return journeys a day before the Great War to ten during the late 1930s. During the mid 1950s British Railways, seeking economies of operation for many secondary lines, introduced two-car multiple-unit diesel trains and then, in 1958, four-wheeled railbuses; with the latter the daily service increased to eighteen return journeys. However, hopes that this might prove to be the line's salvation were ill-founded, a story repeated so often elsewhere, and the Beeching Report of 1963 recommended the line for closure. Little time was lost in ending the passenger service which ceased in September 1964, goods traffic outliving it by less than two years, the final end coming on 18 April 1966.

However, the line from Witham to Braintree has survived to become part of the present railway network, with an hourly passenger service between the junction and the growing town of Braintree. It has even acquired a new station, named Braintree Freeport, just beyond the second station (see Bishop's Stortford – Braintree section).

Wivenhoe – Brightlingsea

Passenger service withdrawn   15 June 1964   *Stations closed*   *Date of closure*
Distance   5 miles   Brightlingsea *   15 June 1964
Companies   Wivenhoe & Brightlingsea Railway

* Closed between 1 February and 7 December 1953.

Brightlingsea Station, *c.* **1910.**

Brightlingsea is a small coastal town situated between the estuaries of the rivers Colne and Stour, the area known from Saxon times as the Tendring Hundred. Railways arrived in that part of Essex with the construction of the Tendring Hundred Railway from Hythe as far as Wivenhoe in 1863, the line being extended westwards to meet the Ipswich – London main line in 1866 and eastward to Weeley in the same year. The line was further extended eastwards until it reached Clacton-on-Sea in 1882.

Locomotive No. 65432 takes on water in preparation for taking the
4.48 train to Colchester from Brightlingsea Station, July 1956.

The line to Brighlingsea was planned as the Wivenhoe & Brightlingsea Railway, a bill being presented to Parliament in 1860, although financial difficulties prevented the five miles of line opening until 18 April 1866. From the outset the Great Eastern worked the line, finally absorbing it 25 years later. Perhaps the financial problems which beset the original works were a harbinger of misfortune; the station at Brightlingsea burned down on the last day of 1901, apparently unmourned by local people who had suffered all kinds of discomforts from the weather while waiting in its bleak and isolated precincts for trains to pick their way along the waterside from the junction. Passenger traffic was such that from 1922 the signalling was removed and the line worked on the 'one engine in steam' principle. Goods traffic, aided by shipbuilding in Brightlingsea and a good trade in oyster fishing was encouraging, but Brightlingsea never achieved the same success as a seaside resort that Walton-on-the-Naze and Clacton enjoyed as a result of the railway (Clacton even managed to sustain a Pullman train service, the Clacton Belle during the 1920s). In 1922 there were nine return journeys on the line daily, mostly worked through from Colchester main line station but two from St Botolph's, a station nearer to the centre of the town. During the 1930s there were ten daily return trips and the line benefitted from day trippers from London looking for a day's sea air.

Traffic was still adequate enough in the post-war era to prevent British Railways closing the line after extensive damage to the track caused by the disastrous east coast floods of January 1953 – though the fact that the idea was proposed suggests all was not well. Even so, it was December 1953 before services resumed. Multiple-unit diesel trains displaced steam working during the 1950s, but these could not save the line from the attentions of the Beeching Report of 1963, which suggested that passenger numbers were less than a third of what was estimated to be needed to ensure its survival. Closure to all traffic came from 14 June the following year.

Woodham Ferrers – Maldon

Passenger service withdrawn	10 September 1939
Distance	8 ¾ miles
Companies	Great Eastern Railwa

Stations closed	*Date of closure*
Stow St Mary *	10 September 1939
Cold Norton	10 September 1939
Baron's Lane **	10 September 1939
Maldon West Halt ***	10 September 1939
Maldon East & Heybridge ****	7 September 1964

* Opened on 24 September 1928.
** Opened on 10 July 1922.
*** Originally named Maldon West until closure on 22 May 1916. Reopened and renamed on 1 August 1919.
**** Originally named Maldon; named Maldon East from 1 October 1889 to 1 October 1907.

Cold Norton Station.

Baron's Lane Halt after the tracks were lifted.

The opening of the London, Tilbury & Southend Railway's line to Southend in 1856 introduced an independent company into East Anglia which was to retain its distinctive character until nationalisation in 1948 and later still. As the Great Eastern emerged by amalgamations, its hold over the eastern counties grew and the continued independence of the LT&SR was all the more marked. During the late 1860s the GER had an opportunity to acquire the Tilbury line but failed to take advantage of it (a failure it came to regret, not least after 1912 when the Midland Railway acquired the LT&SR). To add insult to injury, the Great Eastern's ability to reach Southend via the Tilbury line was thwarted during the early 1880s and this led to a resolve to construct a route of its own. This line, from Shenfield through Wickford and Southminster, opened to Southend on 1 October 1889.

On the same day that the Great Eastern reached Southend, it also opened a second branch to Maldon, this time from Woodham Ferrers from where it struck off for eight miles to join the line from Witham just outside Maldon. Despite such lavish railway provision, Maldon resolutely refused to grow or develop and the second line prospered much less than the first. It may be that at the time Maldon was simply too remote to benefit from the upsurge in residential development and the commuter traffic to London which went with it, but the port had suffered from lack of trade caused by restrictions in the size of vessels which could use it and this was probably the underlying root of decline.

The line's fortunes diminished during the inter-war period despite the London & North Eastern Railway opening two halts, at Stow St Mary and Baron's Lane, to encourage further traffic. In 1938 there were seven return journeys a day from Woodham Ferrers, all connecting with trains to and from London, but a week after the outbreak of war, on 10 September 1939, the passenger service was suspended, never to be resumed. Goods traffic also declined to the point where, after the Shenfield line electrification in 1949, it was used to store redundant rolling stock. The official date of final closure was April 1953, though apparently the redundant vehicles were not removed for scrapping for a further three years.

Stations closed on lines still open to passengers

Canning Town – Stratford

Stations closed	Date
Stratford Market *	6 May 1957

* Originally Stratford Bridge, then Stratford Market (West Ham); line is now part of the Docklands Light Railway and the station was reopened in 2010 as Stratford High Street.

Colchester – Walton-on-the-Naze

Stations closed	Date
Thorington	4 November 1957

Fenchurch Street – Southend

Stations closed	Date
Becontree *	1962 (exact date uncertain)
Dagenham East *	1962
Hornchurch *	1962

* Replaced for stopping services by adjacent stations on the London Transport District line

Fenchurch Street – Southend via Tilbury

Stations closed	Date
Low Street	5 June 1967

Low Street Station, September 1956.